Endorsement...

I highly recommend this book. It is the first time I have read a book about the Creation, good and evil, and suffering, in the context of evangelism and missions. The author has clearly made his case for the fact that God's purpose for Cosmos is to have a viable relationship with every person on earth.

Dr. Carrigan reveals the concepts of good and evil and suffering based upon his own experience, as opposed to fashioning them from theory or mental exercise. It is easy to see that the stresses and strains of the author's life have made him much stronger in his beliefs and actions. He knows God as his Creator, Jesus as his Savior, and the Holy Spirit as his indwelling guide for life.

Reading this book will teach you to trust, or reinforce the trust you already have, in Holy God to be Good and Faithful to you.

> Bill Graham
> Associate Pastor of Missions and Ministry
> First Baptist Church
> Clarksville, Tennessee

God's Purpose in Creation

Vernon M. Carrigan, M.D.

Copyright © 2013 by Vernon M. Carrigan, M.D.

All rights reserved. No part of this book may be used, reproduced, stored in a retrieval system, or transmitted in any form whatsoever — including electronic, photocopy, recording — without prior written permission from the author, except in the case of brief quotations embodied in critical articles or reviews.

All scripture quotations, unless otherwise indicated, are taken from the *Holy Bible, King James Version. KJV.* Public Domain.

FIRST EDITION

ISBN: 978-1-936989-91-1

Library of Congress Control Number: 2013901038

Published by
NewBookPublishing.com, a division of Reliance Media, Inc.
515 Cooper Commerce Drive, #140, Apopka, FL 32703
NewBookPublishing.com

Printed in the United States of America

Reliance Media

Dedications

To my loving late wife,

Melynda Faye Collins Carrigan, 1953-1987.

To Alice Ruth Collins Carrigan, my wonderful wife, who was and is a most precious gift sent from God during the deepest valley of my life, and through whom God has showered His grace and love and healing into my life.

Introduction

Have you ever gazed at the wonder of a clear, starry night or the majesty of a sunny autumn day with its golden array of myriad brilliant colors? What about the miracle of a newborn baby? Have you then wondered how and why it all came to be? Surely, we have all marveled at God's Creation. Some claim that the wonders which we see, feel, smell and taste all happened by chance; but we must believe Paul's writings in the Bible. In Romans and Colossians, Paul writes that we should see God in His Creation and know that it was all spoken into being, both the visible and the invisible, through God's Word, Jesus Christ. Indeed as science, through the study of the Creation, makes more of the invisible become visible and understandable, it seems we come to see God's imprint and perhaps purpose more clearly and definitively every day.

From the most distant stars, galaxies and black holes down to the quarks which hold atoms together, and even light itself by which we see, God created it all – including man in His own image. Why man? According to the Bible, man was created by God to oversee it all and to be God's companion – Adam and Eve walked and talked with God in the beauty of the garden of Creation.

But man disobeyed God. He sinned, and fell into the

damnation of an eternally broken relationship with God and thus was doomed to spiritual and physical death. There was seemingly no solution or salvation for mankind, either as individuals or as a race. Nor was there solution or salvation for the Creation, as it was also cursed by man's sin. For God, perfectly holy and just, must always punish and condemn sin and the sinner.

However, God in His infinite wisdom, grace and mercy did have a plan. He sent His own Son, Jesus Christ, by whom He had created all things, into the world to legally die as the spotless and innocent Lamb on our behalf, thus recreating and regenerating us. Christ has bought us out of the slavery of sin with His own precious blood and made us God's redeemed children and heirs and joint heirs with Himself in His glory.

And when our redemption is made complete in heaven, to wit, the glorification of our bodies, we will live with God and Christ and worship God our Father forever and ever. Moreover, we will exist in heaven as the Bride and body of Christ and as a part of Him as His spotless Church. And it will all be for the Father's glory!

But this begs the eternal question, why does God allow the suffering and evil which exist today, even affecting His beloved children? Why, indeed, are there homicides, infanticides, genocides, divorces, cancer, starvation and so many other such horrible situations and events that go on and on? Why does a loving God allow these awful things to continue in His Creation? Likewise why does God seemingly allow the wicked to prosper?

We learn in the Bible, particularly in Romans, that our redemption is not yet complete, and that the Holy Spirit comforts us in this life. Indeed, if we are joint heirs with Christ in His glory, Paul also declares that we are joint heirs in His suffering in this earthly life. The idea emerges that God's primary plan for this age, the Church age, is for as many lost souls as He chooses to personally believe in His Son for their salvation and thus be added to God's eternal family. Then the ultimate glory and eternity of heaven will come at God's chosen time.

We must realize God is perfectly complete in Himself, but for His own reasons and within His own wisdom He chose to create man as His companion. And consider that if a newly created not-yet-fallen man was a good companion for God, then how much better will redeemed man fulfill this role! This is what Paul is speaking of when he states that the suffering of the present time does not deserve to be compared to the glory which shall be revealed in God's children.

Knowledge of these facts leaves us as Christians today with a clear and definite command to carry out the great commission of our Lord by taking this Good News of the Gospel to a lost and perishing world.

Without a doubt, much of this is still only known and understood by God, remaining a mystery to us. Please come and join me now as we attempt to more closely examine and ponder these questions, hoping to shred the shroud of mystery which surrounds them.

Table of Contents

Chapter 1	Why and How	11
Chapter 2	In the Beginning	17
Chapter 3	Sin, the Fall and the Curse	27
Chapter 4	Redemption and Reconciliation	33
Chapter 5	The Age of Suffering and Grace and Commission – Part One	45
Chapter 6	The Age of Suffering and Grace and Commission – Part Two	57
Chapter 7	God's Ultimate Purpose in Eternity	67
Chapter 8	Personal Application	79
Chapter 9	God's Blessings	87

Chapter 1

Why and How

[8] "For my thoughts are not your thoughts, neither are your ways my ways, saith the LORD. [9] For as the heavens are higher than the earth, so are my ways higher than your ways, and my thoughts than your thoughts."

Isaiah 55:8-9

April 22, 1987, dawned as a perfect day for me. I was blessed by the grace of God with a wonderful wife of eleven years, Melynda, and two delightful children, David, 7, and Jonathan, 4. My medical practice, which I loved, was thriving with wonderful patients and a great staff. I was also blessed with a wonderful extended family and a great network of friends.

So when the sun rose on that beautiful spring morning, all was right with the world. As I kissed Melynda goodbye for the day, I was really kissing her for the last time, it was our last moment together on earth. In a matter of hours, my world was about to change forever.

Unknowing what my future held, I continued with my

perfect day by proceeding to the hospital to make my morning rounds. Melynda would soon be leaving the house to drive the kids to school. About 8 a.m., I received a phone call that no one ever wants to receive. "Dr. Carrigan," a voice said, "your family has been involved in a severe wreck on the bypass and your wife is critical as is one son, but the other son is okay." Stunned and horrified, I rushed to the ER.

Melynda was rolled in on a gurney and I mustered the courage to approach her, as there was no other doctor there. I could see that she was in shock from blood loss, and obviously dying. I had already prayed God's will be done for her, and I knew she was in His hands. The surgeon soon arrived and, with my permission, she was whisked away for emergent, desperate surgery. I was trapped in an overwhelming whirlwind of events beyond my control, but I knew my God was there with me!

David also arrived on a gurney and, although he was pale, he appeared stable. As it turned out, he only had a broken arm and a concussion, but would be watched in the neuro-trauma unit for two days, ultimately making a full recovery.

As was originally reported to me, Jonathan was fine. He arrived at the ER in the arms of a friendly policeman who had been sent by God to minister to him. I later learned over the years, that there were several other kind people who attended to my family that morning.

After Melynda was taken into surgery, I was alone for only a few minutes before several of my nursing friends took me into their proverbial arms and showered their love upon me. I soon began making calls to family and friends. When they arrived, we prayed and waited, fearing the worst while hoping for the best. In my clinical mind, I knew what the outcome would be, but I was hoping to be wrong. After almost two hours of surgery, the surgeon explained that he had done all he could. Melynda's internal injuries were too severe and she had lost too much blood to survive.

My beloved wife had died. WHY? What had happened to cause such a thing? I was told she had pulled out of a side road into the path of a truck, but I would never know the answer as to why she did that. What I struggled most to understand was why my loving heavenly Father, whom Melynda had served with such fervor all of her short life, would allow such a thing to happen.

Shortly thereafter, as I gazed down at her body, I had an indescribable peace knowing she was in the presence of God in heaven and that this was God's plan for her. He surely also must have a plan for me and my children. And, indeed, He did.

The next day, my new faith and peace would be sorely tested as I would have to tell David of his mother's death and what that meant for her and him. God was with us in that moment, the most difficult time in my entire life.

This, of course, is an example of tragedy in my own life. We all experience similar tragedies, as no one is immune. Not only do we suffer accidental death, divorce, financial ruin and devastating sickness, things in large measure beyond our control, but we also suffer the worst evil Satan can mete out, and that mankind can perpetrate on his fellow man: murder, rape, infanticide, genocide and all the rest, including the crusades and the inquisitions which were the works of God's own Church.

Indeed, why does a loving God allow such tragedy to occur? What is his ultimate purpose in this? Even though He does not prevent it, how and, more to the point, *will* He comfort us in the midst of it?

If "WHY" is the greatest question mankind has of God,

surely "HOW" and others which are related are the second greatest. How was the universe formed? Was it by chance or was it by a Creator's choice? What was and is the Creator God's purpose in the Creation? What is the nature of God? What was, is, and will be man's relationship with God? How does that relationship relate to God's ultimate purpose, including His allowing suffering in our lives today?

We shall attempt to examine the answers to these and other questions as we proceed, by using the Bible as the ultimate authority but also using science and experience as corroborating vehicles. Even so, we must remember, as the Bible says, God's ways are higher than our ways and His thoughts are higher than our thoughts so to some extent, the answers will remain shrouded in mystery.

God has promised that when we get to heaven, we will know even as we are known. He will then completely shred the shroud of the mysteries of this life, but in the meantime, He has blessed us with minds with which we can question and explore. Question and explore we shall.

Life Changes

Grains of sand,
Time after time,
Flowing in and out with the tides.
Ever changing, never resting
From eternity past
Into eternity future.

Leaves and trees,
Year after year,
Growing and maturing with the seasons.
Ever changing, never resting
From eternity past
Into eternity future.

Raindrops and snowflakes,
Season after season,
No two ever alike.
Ever changing, never resting
From eternity past
Into eternity future.

Men and women,
Life after life,
Growing and learning with the tides.
Ever changing, never resting
From eternity past
Into eternity future.

The hand of God,
Eon after eon,
Directing time and tide.
Never changing, never resting
From eternity past
Into eternity future.

Mike Carrigan
09-02-2002

Chapter 2

In the Beginning

16"For by him were all things created, that are in heaven, and that are in earth, visible and invisible, whether they be thrones, or dominions, or principalities, or powers: all things were created by him, and for him: 17 And he is before all things, and by him all things consist."

Colossians 1:16-17

Most scientific authorities currently believe and hold that the universe exploded into existence in the Big Bang. Just before the beginning, all of the matter and energy of the universe existed in a singularity, an infinitesimally small point, i.e., the mother of all black holes.

The chief evidence of this is the fact that all observed light has a red Doppler shift, which means that the points from which the light emanated are moving away from the common point of observation, i.e., the Earth. Thus, by deduction, all of the various points of emanation are moving continuously further apart. This means the entire universe is continuously expanding; so if one then extrapolates back to the beginning, the beginning must have been a single point. The other major evidence supporting the Big Bang theory is the existence of the background radiation caused by the initial event.

No one knows the state of things prior to the existence of the singularity or the real nature of it or where it came from, but what about the future? Given that the universe is expanding (some believe ever more slowly), will it continue to expand forever or will the central mass and its gravity ultimately overcome the momentum of the outward expansion and cause a collapse back into a singularity? And could another Big Bang occur with yet another cycle, or have there been an infinite number of cycles already with infinite others yet to occur? No one knows.

Scientists theorize subsequent to our current Big Bang, the matter and energy, including light, were exploded outward, with some coalescing into hydrogen stars in whose nuclear furnaces heavier elements were formed. These in turn were emitted into the void of space, later forming into planets with water and gaseous atmospheres essential for life. Within this environment over the eons of time and by chance, the elements coalesced to form amino acids and nucleic acids, the very building blocks of life. Ultimately, these compounds of amino acids and nucleic acids were able to form structural and regulatory proteins within a package of life, which in turn was capable of reproducing itself with its proteins and acids.

Over the next few billion years on Earth, these primitive packages of life, through the process of biological evolution, became self-contained single cells and then multi-cell, multi-organ complex organisms. Ultimately, these cells evolved into humankind with minds not only able to ask questions such as "why" and "how", but also capable of pondering the answers.

The Bible, however, declares that in the beginning, Jehovah, God, created everything by speaking His Word, Jesus Christ, into the void of absolute nothing, or the "face of the deep".

From **Genesis 1**:

[1] *"In the beginning God created the heaven and the earth.* [2] *And the earth was without form, and void; and darkness was upon the face of the deep. And the Spirit of God moved upon the face of the waters.*

[3] *"And God said, 'Let there be light: and there was light.'* [4] *And God saw the light, that it was good: and God divided the light from the darkness.* [5] *And God called the light Day, and the darkness he called Night. And the evening and the morning were the first day.*

[6] *"And God said, 'Let there be a firmament in the midst of the waters, and let it divide the waters from the waters.'* [7] *And God made the firmament, and divided the waters which were under the firmament from the waters which were above the firmament: and it was so.* [8] *And God called the firmament Heaven. And the evening and the morning were the second day.*

[9] *"And God said, 'Let the waters under the heaven be gathered together unto one place, and let the dry land appear: and it was so.'* [10] *And God called the dry land Earth; and the gathering together of the waters called the Seas: and God saw that it was good.* [11] *And God said, 'Let the earth bring forth grass, the herb yielding seed, and the fruit tree yielding fruit after his kind, whose seed is in itself, upon the earth: and it was so.'* [12] *And the earth brought forth grass, and herb yielding seed after his kind, and the tree yielding fruit, whose seed was in itself, after his kind: and God saw that it was good.* [13] *And the evening and the morning were the third day.*

[14] "And God said, 'Let there be lights in the firmament of the heaven to divide the day from the night; and let them be for signs, and for seasons, and for days, and years: [15] And let them be for lights in the firmament of the heaven to give light upon the earth: and it was so.' [16] And God made two great lights; the greater light to rule the day, and the lesser light to rule the night: he made the stars also. [17] And God set them in the firmament of the heaven to give light upon the earth, [18] And to rule over the day and over the night, and to divide the light from the darkness: and God saw that it was good. [19] And the evening and the morning were the fourth day.

[20] "And God said, 'Let the waters bring forth abundantly the moving creature that hath life, and fowl that may fly above the earth in the open firmament of heaven.' [21] And God created great whales, and every living creature that moveth, which the waters brought forth abundantly, after their kind, and every winged fowl after his kind: and God saw that it was good. [22] And God blessed them, saying, 'Be fruitful, and multiply, and fill the waters in the seas, and let fowl multiply in the earth.' [23] And the evening and the morning were the fifth day.

[24] "And God said, 'Let the earth bring forth the living creature after his kind, cattle, and creeping thing, and beast of the earth after his kind: and it was so.' [25] And God made the beast of the earth after his kind, and cattle after their kind, and every thing that creepeth upon the earth after his kind: and God saw that it was good.

[26] "And God said, 'Let us make man in our image, after our likeness: and let them have dominion over the fish of the sea, and over the fowl of the air, and over the cattle, and over all the earth, and over every creeping thing that creepeth upon the earth.' [27] So God created man in his own image, in the image of God created he

him; male and female created he them. [28] And God blessed them, and God said unto them, 'Be fruitful, and multiply, and replenish the earth, and subdue it: and have dominion over the fish of the sea, and over the fowl of the air, and over every living thing that moveth upon the earth.'

[29] "And God said, 'Behold, I have given you every herb bearing seed, which is upon the face of all the earth, and every tree, in the which is the fruit of a tree yielding seed; to you it shall be for meat. [30] And to every beast of the earth, and to every fowl of the air, and to everything that creepeth upon the earth, wherein there is life, I have given every green herb for meat:' and it was so.

[31] "And God saw everything that he had made, and, behold, it was very good. And the evening and the morning were the sixth day."

And, from **John 1**:

[1] "In the beginning was the Word, and the Word was with God, and the Word was God. [2] The same was in the beginning with God. [3] All things were made by him; and without him was not any thing made that was made. [4] In him was life; and the life was the light of men."

Therefore, one after the other, God created the universe and the Earth with its seas and dry lands and all of its creatures, including man; and He set man in dominion over all of it. He finally declared, "It is very good." He then rested from His work.

Paul writes in Colossians, Chapter 1 that Christ is the image of God the Father of all Creation, both the visible and the invisible, and that all things were created through Him and for Him.

And, finally, the author of Hebrews writes in Chapter 1

that God by Christ made the worlds and that all things are upheld (sustained) by the power of His Word.

These then are the two notions prevalent today concerning the beginning: a purposeless spontaneous explosion with evolution by chance, and a Creation of a Creator God with a purpose. Each view certainly has its staunch supporters and they are thought to be mutually exclusive by most. The creation view was predominant in Western thought until the Enlightenment, and in this post-modern world, the former view has become so.

The view held by an individual and a society becomes very important in practical ways, as the creation view places God at the center of an individual's values and of society's values, both of which are guided by the absolute truths of the Bible; whereas the other view places man at the center of value systems, thus making truth relative and subject to the whim and perspective of the individual. This clash of foundational values and truth then has become the epicenter of most of our societal debates today, including those debates in which the sanctity of human life is involved.

Each individual must make a choice by faith (whether or not he knows to call it faith) to invest in one of these belief systems, as there is no definitive proof of either. Romans, Chapter 1 does warn, however, that man should not only be able to see God in His Creation but also will be held accountable for doing so. *The choice we make on this issue then becomes the defining moment in our individual lives*, and as go individuals so goes society as a whole.

However, the two views on the beginning, in my opinion, are not necessarily mutually exclusive. Many experts have attempted to reconcile the two with significant success. It seems the events of the Big Bang, with the first appearance of light and later of coalesced matter, are not inconsistent with the events of Genesis, Chapter 1. Likewise, a Creator may very well have utilized some form of chemical and biological evolution (although certainly not strictly Darwinian) in the creation of the various forms of life present on the earth today.

Furthermore, new insights from quantum theory and chaos theory paint a picture which is not as rigid in the thought of the future being totally predetermined by the past and present as previously believed. In other words, the possibility of various futures lends more room for the existence of a Creator who would have the prerogative of imposing His will on it, as would also be the case of creatures created by the Creator with free will.[1]

And as Yogi Berra said, "The future ain't what it used to be."

Moreover, one of the other corollaries of the theory of quantum mechanics is that matter does not exist in a single concrete reality, but rather is a complex cloud of mathematical probabilities or possibilities which collapse into one single reality only when observed by a reasoning intelligent being.[1] Wow! How consistent that is with Genesis, considering that God placed mankind in charge of the Creation! At the end of Creation, God said, "It is very good." And indeed it was, but what went wrong? Creating man in the Garden of Eden was only the beginning of man's possibilities. He, of course, sinned and fell from his right relationship with God. Then there is the spiritual parallel of God sending his Son, Jesus, to die for us. In essence, Christ's sacrifice for us collapsed our many possibilities of existence into the one reality of our salvation or restoration of correct relationship with God the Father.

This leads us into our next subject: sin, the fall and the curse.

---

[1] Polkinhorne, Science and Providence: God's Interaction with the World, Templeton Foundation Press

Finding God at the Matterhorn

Oh God;
How my soul
Searches for You
In the midst
Of life's long, dark night.

I remember Your Word;
How You can be seen
In the things
Created by You:
Both visible and invisible.
Your life-giving light,
Reflected from the face
Of the great Matterhorn,
Mirrors your countenance
Into my soul.

The snow and the glaciers
And the cragged face
Of the magnificent mount
Reveal the imprint
Of Your mighty hand.

The verdant trees
And the pointed peaks
And the deep blue, starry sky
Direct my eyes
Toward Your throne.

The glowing face of my beloved
And the fellowship
Of my friends
Warm my heart
With Your love.

Oh, Lord!
You have created it all
With the Word of Your mouth,
Speaking it
Into the vast void of nothing.

Thank You for creating me
And placing me
Within Your will and beauty.
With the words of my mouth
Will I praise You forever!

Mike Carrigan,
On tour with Ruth in Europe
At Zermatt, Switzerland
7-11-11

Chapter 3

Sin, the Fall and the Curse

[12] *"Wherefore, as by one man sin entered into the world, and death by sin; and so death passed upon all men, for that all have sinned."*

Romans 5:12

As we saw in the last chapter, God created the universe, the earth and the fullness thereof and placed man (Adam and Eve) in dominion over it. The Creation was very good in the mind of God, and man walked in unity and friendship with Him. There was no sin, sorrow, sickness, death, grief or decay; only the bliss of knowing and working with God within a perfect relationship.

The relationship was certainly one between Creator and creature, *not* one of puppeteer and puppet. God gave man a free will with which to choose between good and evil; obedience and rebellion. Unfortunately, man, with the assistance of Satan, chose evil and rebellion – sin.

This original sin legally and almost forever broke the perfect relationship between God and man, bringing upon mankind the wrath of a perfectly holy and just God. This left God no choice but to mete out the judgments of physical and spiritual death upon mankind, including all of the woes and evils listed in the first chapter. This judgment applied not only to Adam and Eve, but also to all of their descendants (Romans, Chapter 5) and the Creation itself (Romans, Chapter 8). In other words, man and the Creation were doomed to decay from the perfect state in which they were created by God.

There is a parallel thought within the laws of thermodynamics relative to Creation and the fall and the curse. The first law of thermodynamics states the concept of the conservation of energy and matter: within a closed system, neither matter nor energy is either created or destroyed, but only transformed from one state (of being) to another. The second law states that in these transformations, the dispersion of energy and matter within this system always becomes more random and disordered and less organized, unless energy is applied to the system from another external system, the concept of entropy.

In the beginning, God spoke His all-powerful Word (the incarnation of which is Christ Jesus) into the void of the deep. This spiritual energy brought the universe into being. As God continued to speak over the next seven days, He successively brought into being the order and organization of the highly complex chemical, physical, biological, and societal systems of the Creation, including man. All was perfect as God said, when He saw that it was all very good.

And all would have remained perfect had it not been for the advent of sin. In Genesis, Chapter 3, we learn of man's transgression against God and of man's punishment, the curse, for his sin. The curse is in essence God's unleashing of entropy upon His Creation of perfect systems, bringing disorder, disorganization, death, and decay.

So at this point, we see mankind forever separated from God and doomed to spiritual and physical death because of the disastrous exercise of his free will in sinning. Would the story end there? Thank God, no! Let's go on to the next chapter and see how God begins the process of reconciliation.

Revelation Light

Oh wretched, miserable man,
You have inherited the nature
Of your father, Adam;
And have fallen into
The deep, dark, boiling cauldron
Steaming with the stench of sin,
Forever dead and hopeless,
Permeated by the blackness of night.

But, oh, son of Adam,
I, your heavenly Father
Have loved you forever.
In the dawn of knowledge,
Barely a reflection of My Glory,
You could first see Me
In My Creation,
Wonderful and majestic to behold.

To your father Abraham,
I gave the promise of restoration,
Bridging the wall of separation.
And He pleased Me
With his faith and belief.
To Moses I revealed My Glory
And gave the Law which brought
Enlightenment of the nature of sin.

I, at last, gave Myself,
Through My Son,
My perfect, spotless Lamb,
The fulfillment of the Law.
Through His death and blood
My light now shines
Through the rend in the veil
And into your hearts.

Even now I have shared
My Glory with you
And welcome you
To My throne as sons.
You will be spotless as a Bride
And look into My face
Seeing the fullness of My Glory
Knowing Me as I Am.

My sons, until that day,
You are to share
My living Word and Water
With all mankind,
Shining My light and understanding
Into the darkness of their hearts,
Bringing their souls
From death unto life.

Mike Carrigan
09-09-2005

Chapter 4

Redemption and Reconciliation

[19] *"To wit, that God was in Christ, reconciling the world unto himself, not imputing their trespasses unto them; and hath committed unto us the word of reconciliation."*

2 Corinthians 5:19

God, therefore, would not leave man in the fallen and depraved state into which he had fallen because of his own sin, but rather from before the beginning, God had a plan of redemption and reconciliation. This plan began to unfold with the proto-evangel and was consummated with the death of Christ on the cross. The plan consisted of various stages and revelations or dispensations of God's grace for mankind.

The proto-evangel in Genesis, Chapter 3 was an emphatic statement of God to Satan, but more importantly, it was a covenant between God and Adam and Eve and with their descendants. God stated that from the seed of man, One (Christ) would appear whose heel Satan would bruise, but who would in turn bruise Satan's head. This is the first promise from God of redemption and reconciliation. God soon thereafter established a system of animal sacrifices as He said, "There can be no remission of sin without the shedding of blood." The blood of these spotless animals covered man's sin only temporarily.

Then came the covenant with Abraham, Isaac and Jacob in which He stated that if they would trust God in faith, He would bless them and make their descendants more numerous than the stars in the night sky, and that they would also be a blessing to all of the peoples of the earth. We now understand that God has fulfilled this promise, first with the children of Israel in the Old Covenant and then with Christ and His Church in the New Covenant.

When God led his people out of slavery in Egypt through the Red Sea and the wanderings in the wilderness and finally into the Promised Land, He established a system of laws with them. If perfectly kept, their obedience would lead to individual blessings, but, if broken in any way, their disobedience would lead to individual cursings.

God knew no one would be able to keep these laws. As Paul revealed much later, the law was to serve as a schoolmaster to instruct that no one through his own efforts can be good or holy enough to satisfy a perfectly holy God, who by nature must punish any sin.

Therefore, as part of the legal system, God ordained a complex system of animal blood sacrifices carried out by the Levites, the priestly tribe appointed by God to do so. On the Day of Atonement each year, the high priest would first cleanse himself and then he would take the sacrificed blood for the people into the Holy of Holies. He would take it first in the time of Moses into the tabernacle and in later times into the temple and sprinkle it as a cleansing offering to God on behalf of the people. This offering did not ablate the sins of the people, but merely covered them. And the efficacy of the offering was not permanent, thus the sacrifice and offering had to be repeated yearly.

This offering, not only had the practical cleansing effect for the year, but also and much more importantly, laid the legal foundation for the later sacrifice of Christ for permanent, complete remission of sin.

On the journey from Egypt to the Promised Land, God also gave the people a series of seven feasts or festivals, which were to be observed annually by them and their descendants. These feasts or festivals, which began with Passover and ended with the Festival of Tabernacles, were to serve as a remembrance of God's deliverance of the people from bondage in Egypt. They are also a beautiful foreshadowing of God's deliverance of Adam's entire race from the bondage of sin, beginning with salvation through the blood of Christ, the Christian life including wilderness experiences, the giving of the Holy Spirit, Christ's return for His Church, and the millennial reign of Christ and glory in eternity.

In Romans, Chapter 5, Paul summarized all of this by saying that by Adam and his sin, death came to all, but by Christ, the second Adam, life comes to all.

Upon arrival in the Promised Land, the people were first ruled by God through the office of judges and later through a series of kings. One of these kings was David, a sinful man but at the same time a faithful man, and thus a man after God's own heart. He was of the tribe of Judah, one of Israel's twelve sons. God established a covenant with David in which He promised to raise up a King in David's line who would rule forever sitting on David's throne. This would, of course, be God's own Son, Jesus Christ.

During the several hundred year period of the kings, there were alternating times of relative righteousness, sin, and idolatry. God raised up a series of prophets to instruct the kings and the people in His ways. The prophets also gave a clear message of the birth of Jesus in time and place, and foretold that He would through His death save the people from their sin. Perhaps the most explicit, beautiful and meaningful of these prophesies is found in **Isaiah, Chapter 53:**

[1] "Who hath believed our report? And to whom is the arm of the LORD revealed? [2] For he shall grow up before him as a tender plant, and as a root out of a dry ground: he hath no form nor comeliness; and when we shall see him, there is no beauty that we should desire him. [3] He is despised and rejected of men; a man of sorrows, and acquainted with grief: and we hid as it were our faces from him; he was despised, and we esteemed him not.

[4] "Surely he hath borne our griefs, and carried our sorrows: yet we did esteem him stricken, smitten of God, and afflicted. [5] But he was wounded for our transgressions, he was bruised for our iniquities: the chastisement of our peace was upon him; and with his stripes we are healed. [6] All we like sheep have gone astray; we have turned every one to his own way; and the LORD hath laid on him the iniquity of us all. [7] He was oppressed, and he was afflicted, yet he opened not his mouth: he is brought as a lamb to the slaughter, and as a sheep before her shearers is dumb, so he openeth not his mouth. [8] He was taken from prison and from judgment: and who shall declare his generation? For he was cut off out of the land of the living: for the transgression of my people was he stricken. [9] And he made his grave with the wicked, and with the rich in his death; because he had done no violence, neither was

any deceit in his mouth.

[10] Yet it pleased the LORD to bruise him; he hath put him to grief: when thou shalt make his soul an offering for sin, he shall see his seed, he shall prolong his days, and the pleasure of the LORD shall prosper in his hand. [11] He shall see of the travail of his soul, and shall be satisfied: by his knowledge shall my righteous servant justify many; for he shall bear their iniquities. [12] Therefore will I divide him a portion with the great, and he shall divide the spoil with the strong; because he hath poured out his soul unto death: and he was numbered with the transgressors; and he bare the sin of many, and made intercession for the transgressors."

This message was given to Isaiah by God and recorded 700 years prior to the birth of Christ, and is often referred to as Isaiah's Gospel. Notice the word "satisfied" in Verse 11. The willing sacrifice which Christ made of Himself, God's own Son and a part of the Godhead, Himself, was the only legal mechanism through which the law could be fulfilled for our fallen, guilty race. Nothing else could satisfy God as eternal and holy Judge, nothing else. As Jesus later said, "I am the way, the truth and the life. No one can come to the Father except through Me."

There is no other way to right standing with God except Jesus. Christ later stated that He had not come to destroy the law but to fulfill it. The writer of Hebrews teaches that He did it once and for all, meaning it would never have to be repeated and the New Covenant sealed with His sacrifice is open for all to accept. Paul affirmed this in 2 Corinthians, Chapter 5, in stating that God was in Christ Jesus reconciling the world unto Himself.

Christ, Himself, is also the High Priest of the New Covenant as He presented His own blood to God in the Holy of Holies not in the man-made temple, but in heaven at the very throne of God. And as our new High Priest, He sits at the right hand of God forever making intercession for us.

Even though salvation is open to all under the New Covenant, Jesus informed Nicodemus that one must be born again by believing in Jesus as a personal Savior, and also believing that He took the sins of the individual upon Himself and that God judged Him guilty in the individual's place and that God punished Him in the individual's place. In the words of Jesus, salvation is a matter of believing in Him through personal faith.

Consistent with this is the teaching of Paul in Romans and Galatians that salvation can never be earned by individually fulfilling the law but only through faith in the work of Christ. It is a free gift of God through grace and can never be earned through merit. Paul gives the summation in Romans, Chapter 10 by saying, believing in the heart and confessing with the mouth that Jesus is Lord brings individual salvation.

The essence of salvation is that it restores the broken relationship with God and brings us back into proper fellowship with Him. At the point of our salvation, our spirits are restored and regenerated and made spotless before God, and we are thus righteous again in His sight, although the old sin nature still dwells in our flesh during this life. Our regenerated spirits will live forever with God and Christ.

Additionally, when we die and ultimately go to heaven, we will receive glorified bodies which will never die, but our current earthly bodies will die and are subject to sickness and disease under the curse, as is the Creation still.

Salvation of our souls has to do with sanctification, the lifelong process through which we are to follow the example of

Jesus as in Philippians, Chapter 2, the working out of our salvation as Paul calls it, and the renewing of the mind as Paul refers to it in Romans, Chapter 12. Through this process we are to become more like Christ in humility, service, obedience and by sacrifice. In this life, others are supposed to see Christ in us so that they will seek salvation for themselves. This is God's chief purpose for us as individuals in this life: to become like Christ. It will serve us and our fellow man well here and will please God; but sanctification also prepares us for God's ultimate purpose in our eternal lives with Him in glory, which I shall examine in a later chapter.

Our sanctification is nurtured by the Holy Spirit, as noted above by abiding in Christ and becoming like Him and fruitful in and through Him as seen in John, Chapter 15; but it will be brought to completion and perfection when we truly become one with Him and His Church and the Father as seen in John, Chapter 17. The things of this life will then become truly meaningless and the Father will become all of our meaning and being, as He is for Christ.

We have seen how in the beginning, God spoke the Creation into being and how man brought the curse in the form of entropy upon it. But praise be to God, in His infinite mercy and grace, He chose to speak again, bringing the incarnation of Jesus.

[16] *"For God so loved the world, that he gave his only begotten Son, that whosoever believeth in him should not perish, but have everlasting life.* [17] *For God sent not his Son into the world to condemn the world; but that the world through him might be saved."*
John 3:16-17

This Word of recreation through Christ's blood sacrifice and resurrection has reversed the spiritual and physical entropy of the curse. When lost man accepts Christ as his Savior, the energy of the Word, recreates him spiritually and makes him a new creature. Romans, Chapter 8 then tells us how the physical Creation groans as it awaits Christ's second coming, at which time it will be freed from the curse. We, God's children, will then also be freed from the curse of physical death and decay and the effects of entropy. We will be given glorified bodies and live forever with God and Jesus in heaven, the new Creation.

We must then conclude that according to the very laws of nature, the universe could never have created itself or evolved spontaneously into a lower state of entropy (perfect order), but was indeed created into a state of perfection by the spoken Word of God, bringing its boundless energy into the face of the deep. And afterwards, when mankind brought the curse of entropy upon all of the Creation, including himself, God in His infinite mercy and grace once again spoke his all-powerful Word, negating entropy and bringing in an everlasting perfect recreation.

Having accomplished all of this, the question then becomes, why is God waiting to bring about the consummation of His healing, ending the sickness, grief and evil which still exist on the earth today? I shall address this issue in the next chapter.

The Man

One saw a man with wounds,
Bandages he did supply.

Another saw the bullet holes,
Violence of days gone by.

Another the fear of a little girl,
As tears flowed from her eyes.

Another the spirit of the wounded man,
For whom the Gospel he supplied.

Through us, the man saw The Son,
And asked forgiveness bye and bye.

While The Father asked of all,
"With My law have *you* complied?"

The Savior last of all declared,
"For all, My life,
I freely gave,
That now and for evermore,
They will be known,
As Only Mine!"

Mike Carrigan
06-21-05

The Encounter

Jesse approached us
From across the room,
Cluttered, noisy, dirty,
In the heart of the favela.

On his face
Was the look of worry,
Which foretold his concern,
For physical and spiritual illness.

Forehead furrowed,
Cheeks fallen,
Eyes dull,
Countenance defeated.

His feet were burning
With the pain of disease,
His heart with
The sickness of sin.

Physical illness treated,
We shared God's love with him.
At the name of Jesus,
Tears flowed down his cheeks.

Repentance and Faith
Did their work on his heart
As he prayed for forgiveness
And accepted Christ.

In his eyes now
Was the light of New Life.
His face now glowed
With the smile of God's love.

The love light
Reflected from him to us,
Who had shared with him,
Bringing with it Peace and Joy.

Our souls danced together,
In God's Glory,
The dance of Christian Brotherhood
Which shall last forever.

Mike Carrigan, MD
June, 2003

Chapter 5

The Age of Suffering and Grace and Commission

PART ONE

[4] *"Behold, his soul which is lifted up is not upright in him: but the just shall live by his faith."*
Habakkuk 2:4

[8] *"But ye shall receive power, after that the Holy Ghost is come upon you: and ye shall be witnesses unto me both in Jerusalem, and in all Judaea, and in Samaria, and unto the uttermost part of the earth."*
Acts 1:8

We now re-approach the question which we earlier posed: Why does God allow the continuation of evil and suffering and grief in all of their many pervasive forms?

In more than thirty years of medical practice, I have watched many faithful Christian patients suffer mightily, then die and leave behind grieving families. Why?

I have witnessed other Christian patients suffer financial setbacks and spousal abuse, infidelity, and divorce, and have seen innocent children and the elderly suffer abuse. Why?

I have read of and witnessed natural disasters in which thousands die, sometimes even while at worship in church. Why?

I have read of various forms of one-on-one evil such as robbery, assault, murder, and rape, events in which innocents are injured. Why?

I have read of the heinous acts of the Roman emperors and of men such as Hitler and Stalin and, yes, even of the acts performed in the very name of God by the crusaders and the inquisitors and legalists in the church today. Why?

I have heard of Christians being martyred for their faith both in the past and in other countries today. Why?

I even consider and still grieve over the personal tragedy of my first wife's death and my present wife's continual suffering with pain and severe depression. Why?

At the same time the wicked seem to prosper. Why?

Indeed, why *does* God allow all of this to continue?

When Habakkuk asked the same questions of God centuries ago, God said to him, "The just shall live by faith." This command is reiterated three times in the New Testament. Sometimes, we don't know God's reasons for such things happening, but we must believe by faith that He is allowing what is best for us or, at least, that He *will* comfort and console us in the midst of trials and give us the sustaining grace to endure.

God told Habakkuk that in the end, His justice would be appropriately meted out, and indeed it was. And at the end of this age or dispensation, the Church Age or Age of Grace, when Christ returns, God will again mete out His justice and make things right, and we must believe this by faith.

There are many reasons why God's people and others suffer today. First and foremost, we are still living in physical bodies which are part of the fallen Creation which is still under the curse, and it has been appointed unto all men to die physically. In this life, we are subject to physical law, including entropy with its sicknesses and diseases and even physical accidents or happenstance.

This means that if a young mother such as Melynda pulls her car out in front of an oncoming truck, only something bad can occur. Likewise, if a person is promiscuous, he or she is at risk of contracting certain incurable diseases which can lead to lifelong suffering or even death. And we are all well aware of the dire consequences of smoking and drinking and illicit drugs.

We are also subject to spiritual law; there is still a price to be paid for spiritual disobedience in this life. As an example, Paul cited those who died in the church at Corinth because of their abuse of the Lord's Supper.

We as individuals are also unfortunately subject to the will of others, as previously enumerated by acts of crime, abuse and other atrocities. And we are also vulnerable to the temptation and the will of Satan, as Peter warns us in his epistle. Look at the examples of Job in a positive light and of Judas in a negative light.

God does not interfere with man in the exercise of his free will, except perhaps on rare occasions nor does He countermand spiritual law or physical law except on rare occasion. Why God chooses to miraculously heal some (Hezekiah) or make the sun stand still for one (Joshua) and not for others is a mystery and shall remain so in this life.

And as we have noted, the just shall live by faith; and whatever the circumstance, we must believe that in the context of

Romans 8:28, *For those who love God and are called according to His purpose, God ultimately works it out for the good, and if not here in this life, ultimately in heaven.* This comes about, I believe, in our lives if we are truly seeking God's will; our will and His will come together, under the power of the Holy Spirit, in some miraculous, marvelous, and mysterious way. This transaction often occurs through faith and prayer, because prayer and faith together form the key to unlocking the mystery of God's will for us, both for understanding and taking action.

Moreover, at the beginning of this age when Jesus left the disciples behind, He commanded them to spread the good news of the Gospel and the invitation of salvation around the world; to make disciples in all nations and kindreds of people. Christ will not return until this occurs.

It becomes evident that God's primary will for this age is to have as many lost souls as possible choose to accept Jesus as their Lord and Savior, thus completing the size and numbers in the Church as the Father has preordained. If God had ended the age immediately before Christ ascended into heaven, only the original believers would be in the Church. Likewise, if Christ had returned 1000 years later, none of us who are alive today would be in the Church, and indeed we would never have been born physically, let alone reborn spiritually. No, God will call an end to the age and send Christ back for the Church only when His plan is complete.

Beyond this, if God presently did away with all suffering, evil and grief, He would in essence be ablating lost man's free will in choosing Christ as his Lord unto salvation. This would, of course, contradict His primary purpose in growing the Church during this age.

Our (the Church) primary mission in this life is to carry out the

Great Commission as the Lord commanded and to be ambassadors for God in this endeavor as Paul cites in 2 Corinthians, Chapter 5. It seems that all too often in the Church today; especially in America, Christians place their own comfort ahead of the Great Commission, wasting the God-given days of life.

Paul speaks of following the example of Christ in Philippians, Chapter 3, when he cites that he knows Christ in His resurrection and in the fellowship of His sufferings and in conforming to His death. Paul counts it as all gain that he has given up the comforts of this world in exchange for living the Christ-centered and Christ-following life. God has richly supplied all of his needs in a way which was not understood by the world or many in the Church of his day or in our own today.

James, in Chapter 1, exhorts us to count it all joy when life's trials test our faith, bringing patience and completeness to our spiritual lives. There is no doubt that the desert experiences are the ones which bring us closer to God. They take us beyond the bounds of our human wisdom and capability and into the arms of God and His capability, which is boundless. Such was the case for me upon Melynda's death. Just as sure is the fact that often times, God uses the crises of life to take us from one zone of comfort into a new vista, ministry or life stage.

Christ commands us to take up our cross daily and to follow Him and be yoked to Him for doing His work. But how many of us understand and how many of us will follow? Christ did not give His life to ensure our earthly comfort, but rather to enable our own salvation, and He has now entrusted us to take the Gospel message to the lost!

I have clearly witnessed this on one of my many mission trips to East Asia. There is quite a contrast between the Church at work there and the Church in America. There was one particular trip in 2006, of which I later wrote, that left the message penetrated deeply into my heart.

"Let us return to September 6, 2006. On this day, I find myself on my third medical mission trip to East Asia with my wife, three dear friends and fellow travelers. Today, we have ministered to the people of "JD", a village remote in time, society, and spirit.

Indescribable and unimaginable trash, filth, poverty, and illness abound as we care for the imprisoned, oppressed souls who live there in a dark pagan temple made of wood with dirt floors. A higher official is angry with the local leader because he has allowed foreigners into the village without the official's knowledge. And so it goes on and on and on, miserably and endlessly.

In my quiet time following lunch, I am compelled to pray that God will loosen the bonds with which the villagers have been enslaved by Satan and his minions.

As we return to our "home" that afternoon, the Holy Spirit begins to speak to me and enlighten me through my recent studies in Hebrews and Henry Drummond's "The Programme of Christianity,"[2] which I am continuing to read on the bus. Drummond eloquently writes of human suffering and sorrow, which come not so much from the way men die but rather from the way they live and are forced to live. He further states that some men live and exist in hellish prisons where no breath of heaven ever reaches, where social soils exist in which only sin and unrighteousness can grow and flourish. He declares that these systems must be destroyed and the captives set free!

Moreover, he opines that wherever the poor are trodden upon or tread upon each other; wherever the air is poison and the water foul; wherever want stares at us, vice reigns, and rags rot – there is where

---

[2] Collins World Press

the Avenger (God and His arm, The Church) must take its stand.

One of my spiritual mentors, who handed me the book as we were leaving on our trip, wrote in the margin of this very page that my (our) imminent challenge and calling are the above thoughts. And, indeed, they are the urgent and clarion call of our Lord to His Church today. Do we hear? Do we understand? Will our hearts be stirred? Will we act?

This evening, my friends and I have the privilege of meeting and speaking with a local pastor, a truly first-century type, Holy Spirit-inspired preacher and man of God. He ministers in an unregistered house church and shares with us the stories of his church's trials, tribulations, and personal persecutions.

The authorities have already threatened to close down the Sunday school, but were thwarted by the Holy Spirit's miraculous intervention in confusing, thus preventing the children from identifying their teachers.

The pastor was detained, questioned, threatened, and forbidden to hold further open assemblies and evangelize. Under this pressure, the Holy Spirit gave him the courage and faith to refuse, both verbally and in writing, to promise the same; and he actually shared the Gospel with them. We could see the light of the Holy Spirit in his countenance as he related this story. Paul and Silas must have looked the same way as they walked out of their prison!

In spite of all this, the congregation spiritually flourishes and has grown to several thousand members. But now, it must break up into several hundred cells and face the daunting task of training hundreds of new leaders.

One must ask, how does the present-day church in America compare with this shining example? It seems we build cathedrals and our personal barns and study theories of theology and worship; but *our buildings are cold, there is too little empathy for the lost, too little true worship, and too little joy in our hearts as we rest in our artificial comfort.*

And the God-given days of opportunity in our lives slip away one by one, just as the dead leaves of autumn fall from fruitless trees to the cold, hard ground.

The writer of Hebrews instructs us to move beyond our complacency and the foundational tenets of our faith, and thus begin using the Gospel as the daily signpost of our lives. He also challenges us to leave our milk behind and to begin eating the meat of evangelism and discipleship in these last days.

May we remain diligent in finishing the race which our Lord has set before us, so that when He returns He will say, "Well done my good and faithful servants." Let us continue to keep in step with God's program and together march by faith into His new frontier of missions and with the Holy Spirit be the Avenger of the poor and lost."

This story illustrates God's mission for us in this age – to carry out Christ's Great Commission, working with Him and in the power of the Holy Spirit. When we focus on this, the importance of our own suffering seems perhaps somewhat less important. And as Paul writes in Romans, Chapter 8, "*the sufferings of this present time are not worthy to be compared to the glory which shall be revealed in us*"; not only the glory which shall be revealed in us in heaven in the future, but also the glory which should be reflected by us to those lost and suffering in the world today.

Does God leave us to suffer alone or does He support and comfort us in some way as we live our lives and carry out his work? He certainly does comfort us, and I shall explore this assurance in the next chapter.

The Eyes of Christ on Rio

As I stand astride the mountaintop,
I gaze down on Rio,
The Pearl of Brazil.
I see the spraying surf,
The white sand beaches,
The sheer cliffs,
And the fertile favelan fields,
Who will feed My sheep?
Who will feed My sheep?

As I look onto the teeming streets,
And into the houses,
I see the poverty, the unclothed children,
Physical and mental illness,
And crying mothers.
Who will feed My sheep?
Who will feed My sheep?

As I look upon the hurting faces,
And search the aching hearts
Of my lost people,
I share their pain,
Feel the hardness,
Sense the darkness and hopelessness,
And see the shackles of sin.
Who will feed My sheep?
Who will feed My sheep?

Lord, here am I!
I will share their pain with You.
I will preach to the poor.
I will help You free the captives.
I will bring them Your bread and water.
I will minister to the ill and broken-hearted.
I will be salt and light for them.
Lord, here am I!
Lord, here am I!

Now when I look onto Rio,
I see my light shining into the darkness,
Reflecting off the faces and the mended hearts
Of my people as from a diamond.
Their spirits soar like the pipa.
Now they cry:
We are free!
We are free!

As for me,
The people have become an altar,
As God has used me as His instrument
With my brothers and sisters,
Brazilian and American alike,
I have grown closer to Him,
More sensitive, more humble.
Praise God!
I am Free!
I am Free!

Possa Deus todos nos Libertar.
May God Free Us All!
May God Free Us All!

Mike Carrigan
06-13-2002

Chapter 6

The Age of Suffering and Grace and Commission

PART TWO

² *"Grace be to you, and peace, from God our Father, and from the Lord Jesus Christ."*

Ephesians 1:2

²⁸ *"And we know that all things work together for good to them that love God, to them who are the called according to his purpose."*

Romans 8:28

In the previous chapter, we examined the reasons why God allows suffering and pain and trials and evil to persist. The preservation of man's free will in order to make salvation available to him is the foundational reason. Also, the suffering of the present time is not to be compared with the glory which is to be revealed in us in this life and in heaven. Now, we shall examine how God sustains and supports us in the midst of life's trials.

Let's look to the apostle Paul as an example. In 2 Corinthians, Chapter 12, he writes of his thorn in the flesh, most likely a physical illness or malady or impediment. He earnestly prayed for God to remove this three times and God did not. Immediately prior to this, in Chapter 11, he writes of his sufferings for the Gospel, which included beatings and imprisonments and shipwreck and near-death experiences. God instructed that His grace was sufficient for Paul. This means that in the midst of life's trials, God is with us and gives us His peace, the peace which cannot be explained with human wisdom, as written in Hebrews, Chapter 6.

This grace and peace is the same – whether one is struggling in the general trials of life, in the trials of spreading the Gospel, in the process of wasting and dying from a chronic physical illness or as a Christian martyr. I have personally witnessed numerous examples of this grace and peace in people in all of the above except martyrdom, and I have read accounts of that. It is obvious that the grace and peace of God are palpable and real and sustaining!

In 2 Corinthians, Chapter 6, Paul shares another aspect of this when he describes the heavy external pressures and internal distresses which he bore in the spreading of the Gospel and in the care and support of the Church. He was able to triumphantly endure by the knowledge and pureness and love and patience given to him by the Holy Spirit and by the truth of the Gospel and the power and righteousness of God. As he said, "If God be for us who can be against us?" Indeed, no one!

In a similar passage in Ephesians, Chapter 6, he gives instructions by which we must fight off the attacks of Satan. We must have a thorough knowledge of the truth of the gospel and be sure of the knowledge of our salvation, including the righteousness which God has given us. We must have a strong faith in God's promises and be thoroughly versed in God's living Word, the Bible. The Word of God is the sword of the Spirit, and when we quote the Word of God to Satan, as did Christ in the wilderness, he must flee. The Word of God is the most powerful force in the universe, as it was with this Word by which God spoke everything into existence.

Paul goes on to say that prayer must always be in our hearts, meaning prayer is the key. Too often, we view prayer as a mechanism through which we change God's will to be in line with ours, and on rare occasions, perhaps this is the case. Much more often, however, prayer is the spiritual means through which we bring our will in line with God's, a source of true peace, indeed. At its highest level, according to Polkinghorne[3], prayer becomes an opportunity for our minds and spirits to become one with the Creator of the universe. Wow! How many of us view prayer in this way, and how many of us have participated in such prayer?

I think this entails the relationship with God of which Jesus was speaking in the upper room in John, Chapter 17, when He stated that we should be one with God and Christ, as God and Christ are one with each other. Wow! How can we possibly understand such a relationship with God and possibly begin to live in it? It is only made possible by the power of the Holy Spirit and by completely surrendering our lives to Him, and it is the only real source of peace in this life. But all too often, we allow the phantom pursuits of this world to choke the life from our relationship with God, to our detriment and to His disappointment.

If we could only live this kind of abiding life of which Jesus also spoke in John, Chapter 15, the cares of this world and the trials and sufferings of this world, including even death, would evaporate into nothingness. I will relate a specific and real glimpse of this in

---

[3] Polkinghorne, "Science and Providence: God's Interaction with the World" Templeton Foundation Press

my own life at the beginning of chapter 8.

Now let's go on to examine Romans, Chapter 8, perhaps the greatest chapter of hope and exhortation in the entire Bible. Paul starts by admonishing us to walk in the Spirit and not in the flesh, for those who walk in the Spirit are the sons of God and as sons, we may call God, "Daddy" in the most endearing sense; and in this relationship, we have access to the throne of God, our Father, in prayer and may metaphorically sit in His lap and love Him and present our petitions to Him.

Also as sons, we are joint heirs with Christ in His sufferings and in His glory. What a privilege to suffer with and for Christ, as Paul stated in Philippians, Chapter 3. Wow! We shall reconsider God's glory and how He shares it with us and reveals it through us in the next chapter, as it indeed is absolutely that which justifies Christ's sufferings and our own, and is at the heart of the reason for the Creation.

But Paul goes on to say that suffering will come in this life until we are taken to heaven, and that we must endure it with patience. In the meantime, the Father has sent his Holy Spirit to live within us and to comfort us and lead us. When life is at its hardest and cruelest and we come to a point in which we cannot or know not how to pray for ourselves, the Holy Spirit will pray for us the perfect will of the Father to the Father, thus bringing it to fruition in our lives.

Additionally, Paul reminds us that our High Priest, Jesus Christ, is at the right hand of the Father at His throne in heaven, continually interceding for us.

Indeed if God is for us, who can be against us? For nothing can separate us from God's love. Look at the list:

"Shall tribulation, or distress, or persecution, or famine, or nakedness, or peril, or sword? [36] *As it is written, For thy sake we are killed all the day long; we are accounted as sheep for the slaughter.* [37] *Nay, in all these things we are more than conquerors through him that loved us.* [38] *For I am persuaded, that neither death, nor life, nor angels, nor principalities, nor powers, nor things present, nor things to come,* [39] *Nor height, nor depth, nor any other creature, shall be able to separate us from the love of God, which is in Christ Jesus our Lord."*

Romans 8:35b-39

A similar list is presented by the writer of Hebrews in Chapter 11. Here, the triumphant deeds of the heroes of faith are enumerated, while others are cited as seemingly not having their faith rewarded with success or fruition:

[32] *"And what shall I more say? for the time would fail me to tell of Gedeon, and of Barak, and of Samson, and of Jephthae; of David also, and Samuel, and of the prophets:* [33] *Who through faith subdued kingdoms, wrought righteousness, obtained promises, stopped the mouths of lions,* [34] *Quenched the violence of fire, escaped the edge of the sword, out of weakness were made strong, waxed valiant in fight, turned to flight the armies of the aliens.* [35] *Women received their dead raised to life again: and others were tortured, not accepting deliverance; that they might obtain a better resurrection:* [36] *And others had trial of cruel mockings and scourgings, yea, moreover of bonds and imprisonment:* [37] *They were stoned, they were sawn asunder, were tempted, were slain with the sword: they wandered about in sheepskins and goatskins;*

being destitute, afflicted, tormented; [38] (Of whom the world was not worthy:) they wandered in deserts, and in mountains, and in dens and caves of the earth. [39] And these all, having obtained a good report through faith, received not the promise: [40] God having provided some better thing for us, that they without us should not be made perfect."
Hebrews 11:32-40

This is a very difficult passage to understand and apply. The ones who were positive examples of overcoming faith certainly have received a good report, as their prayers were answered. But the ones who seemingly had not had their prayers answered have also received a good report of their faith, perhaps even an implied higher report or commendation. Somehow, it seems God has answered their prayers and rewarded their faith in the lives of others in the family of God.

Their faith is not to be diminished one iota because of apparent lack of fulfillment, as was the case of Paul in his prayer for healing. Perhaps this is the only thought which may bring peace when life has put us into one of its deepest and darkest pits. God is still there with us, both providing for and delighting in our faith.

Therefore, God has made all provisions for us, not for comfort in this life but for endurance in the race which He has set before us. We have the immediate and imminent support of the entire Godhead as we run and endure and persevere. God indeed will work out all of the challenges and opportunities of life in bringing His will to bear for us if we love Him and seek His will.

This begs the eternal question of on what or in whom can we successfully base our hope in this life and beyond, both as individuals and as a race. Polkinghorne[3] notes that physical eschatology will fail us as the universe as science understands it is doomed to expand either into isolated black holes or perfect randomness (entropy), or to collapse into a singularity, even as it began. Neither of these possibilities is capable of supporting physical life as we know it or of supporting hope in this life or beyond.

I would add that societal eschatology will also fail us in our hope. There are many who believe that man is evolving into a higher state all along; but if we examine experience and history, we surely know this is not the case. We also know from the Bible that mankind is a fallen race and capable of no lasting redeeming and saving act. No, I will not place my hope in fallen man.

Therefore, we must look to a Creator for our hope[3], and we must look beyond a theoretical deist God who has simply created and then has stepped back only to observe without an ultimate purpose for his Creation.

Likewise, we must search beyond a God who has created and then rigidly orchestrates, as a puppeteer, His Creation toward His ultimate purpose. This gives some hope for the future, but little for the present. This is akin to but perhaps just beyond the God of Calvin's theology. I could perhaps trust and worship such a God, but I would find it difficult to truly and completely love and adore him.

Finally, let's consider a God who has not only created and who has an ultimate purpose which He will bring to fruition, but who also, as in Arminian theology, has given created man a free will. He then carefully and lovingly interacts with us, exercising His will, in spite of our often poor decisions of will, to bring about His purpose for our lives here and today, and beyond into glory. This is the grace of which Paul speaks in Romans, Chapter 8; and this is what Romans 8:28 is specifically saying to us; and this is what grace is all about in its fullest meaning. And this is what gives us hope not only for heaven, but also for each and every day of our lives.

Suffering Christian Life

We enter into life
Condemned to die,
All black inside,
And filled with sin.

With life
Comes mirth
Which makes our hearts
Sing with joy.

But joy,
Like our lives,
Is but a vapor
Before the Lord.

Our real purpose
Is of a different sort:
To know Him
And to be saved by His blood.

To suffer
And with Him die to self;
And to bring glory
To God.

He does not leave us
To suffer alone,
But lives in our hearts
Day by day.

Bringing comfort
And real Godly joy
Until we enter into heaven
One day.

'til that time the meaning of our lives
Is growth and fruitfulness
In the context of our physical finiteness
And then into eternal infinity;

Not current comfort
In the context
Of our frailty and finality.

Our lives then are to be
Spent for the glory of God,
And to Him be praise
Forever and for eternity!

Mike Carrigan
7-9-11

Chapter 7

God's Ultimate Purpose in Eternity

> [2] *"Beloved, now are we the sons of God, and it doth not yet appear what we shall be: but we know that, when he shall appear, we shall be like him; for we shall see him as he is."*
>
> 1 John 3:2

We have now studied the Creation, sin, the fall and the curse, and likewise how God has redeemed man through the blood of Jesus and how this sacrifice, when acted upon personally by faith, can bring individual salvation. Moreover, we have considered why God has allowed suffering, pain and evil to continue to exist today and how that is related to his primary will in this age of bringing as many lost souls into the Church as possible.

And lastly, we have studied how He has made provision for our patience and peace and endurance in the face of life's trials, and that it is His will for the individual believer in this age and during his life to become evermore like Jesus in humility, obedience, service and sacrifice, the process of sanctification. Sanctification, which is becoming like Jesus, in some way, then prepares us for the next life.

We learned that we are joint heirs with God's Son, Jesus, and so we are joint heirs not only of His glory but also of His suffering. The suffering of this present time is not worthy to be compared to the glory which shall be revealed in us, both today to the lost and later, in heaven or eternity.

This brings us to another set of questions. First, why did God, who was and is and always shall be perfect in every way within Himself, create the universe with man in it and in charge of it, knowing that man would sin and bring the curse upon it, with all of the untold suffering? Why did He do this, knowing that it would finally require Him to send His own Son to die a horrible death on the cross and bear all of the sin and suffering of the entire race, while isolated and separated from the Father? It certainly is very difficult for the human mind to fathom.

Likewise, what is the nature of the glory we shall have in heaven? It will certainly be grand if it will make us forget all of the suffering of the past – and it will! Now we see God and His ways as through a dark window; but when we are in heaven, we will see Him face to face in all of His glory, and He will teach us His ways and purposes. We will know Him and His ways, even as well as He knows Himself, His Creation and as He knows us. This much we know we are promised, and certainly this much is a good start in glory!

Romans, Chapter 8 does tell us the Holy Spirit is a down payment on this promise. He is here to live within us and to comfort, guide and instruct us and through prayer to have the will of God worked out in our lives. One could surmise that this is a foreshadowing of the perfect peace we shall have in heaven, resting perfectly in God's will and in perfect relationship with Him. The Holy Spirit is leading us toward this in our lives today and is our guide in the path of sanctification.

Let's turn to Scripture for the answers.

In the beginning, God created man in his own image (Genesis 1:26) which in part would mean Adam was a triune being, as are we, like God with a spirit, a soul and a body (1 Thessalonians 5:23 and Hebrews 4:12). The triune parts of God are of course the Father and the Holy Spirit and the physical part, Christ, who later via the incarnation was physically born as a man, the second Adam (Romans, Chapter 5). Jesus is fully God and fully man in the incarnation. In Genesis, Chapter 2, God formed Adam from the dust of the earth and then breathed His own Spirit into Him in order to bring him to life in His own image. Adam was of God and like God before he fell.

Likewise in Genesis, Chapter 2, we read of the perfect fellowship which existed between God and Adam and Eve. Man was a companion and a delight to God, and God was a companion and a delight to man.

As we have seen when Adam sinned and fell, death and the curse came upon him and all of the Creation. God, however, through redemption and salvation, has made regeneration of the spirit and sanctification of the soul and ultimate glorification of the body of man possible. Also even though all men will die physically, spiritual death will not come upon God's children and we will not be forever separated from God, but will live with Him in glory through eternity. That fellowship which existed between God and man will be restored and indeed be richer and fuller with redeemed man than it ever could be with created, unfallen man. Perhaps this is a major reason for God's Creation, the fall and finally redemption.

What are redeemed man's final state and nature and relationship with God to be?

Romans, Chapter 8 states that we are the adopted sons of God, heirs and joint heirs with His only begotten Son, Jesus. As such, we have access to Him at his throne and may even address Him as a child would a loving father, calling Him, "Daddy."

2 Peter 1:4 declares that we, God's children, are partakers of God's divine nature. That is to say, we are as God in His nature which is mirrored by the fruits of the Spirit.

He has given us his own righteousness (2 Corinthians 5:17-21). God through Christ has made us new creatures with His divine nature (prior paragraph) and with His own righteousness.

We are kings and priests unto God serving under the office Of Christ and we shall rule and reign with Him (Revelation 1:6 and 5:12).

The Church is the physical body of Christ and He is the head while we are the members. (1 Corinthians, Chapter 15, Romans, Chapter 12, Ephesians 1:22-23). The Church is also the Bride of Christ and He the head and Husband (Ephesians 5:23, Revelation, Chapters 21 and 22). And upon Christ's harvesting His Church from the world at the end of this age, there will occur in heaven a magnificent marriage between the Lamb, the Bridegroom, and the Church – the Bride. Christ will not only have paid a dowry for His Bride with His blood but also will have redeemed Her from the wages of sin, the blackness of spiritual death ; and He will adorn her in pure white linen. What a celebration it will be!

What can we glean from all of this? Before the Creation, God was perfectly complete in every way and perfectly holy and just. But He desired companionship which He initially found in the garden with Adam and Eve. Then Adam and Eve sinned (which God knew would happen out of their free will, as He did not wish the companionship of puppets or automatons, but of those who would freely choose to be His companions and worship Him), forever breaking the relationship. God so loved man that He over centuries patiently gave a system of laws and entered covenants with man, which culminated in His giving His own Son on the cross for our redemption, reinstating the relationship. After the Church Age, in which He adds redeemed souls to His new family, He will command Christ to harvest His Church from the world to live with Him as His companion in heaven, as He did with Adam and Eve in the garden.

But the new relationship will go well beyond mere companionship. It is God's plan based on the above Scriptures to make us His very children with His own righteousness and divine nature and to rule and reign under Him as kings and priests.

The Church is the body of God's Son, Christ, and Christ is the head and Bridegroom of His Bride, the Church. And finally let's look at John 17: 21-23 once more. Jesus is praying in the upper room, that God makes the members of the Church one, as are Jesus and the Father, and that the Church be one with God and Christ. If the Church is to be one with God and Christ, it becomes quite evident that God's plan is to make the Church, in some marvelous, miraculous, and mysterious way, a part of Himself in order to complete Himself and to make us His perfect companions.

He referred to the original Creation as being very good, and Christ now refers to this new relationship as being perfect. He refers to this new relationship as being glorious, the same glory which God gave to Christ. This is the same glory of which Paul speaks in Romans, Chapter 8, which makes the suffering of this present time vanish in comparison.

For us, the glory of heaven will be so much more than the mansions and streets of gold or even the rest and peace. This is related to the fact that we will be one with God and Christ and rule and reign and govern over the universe forever more!!

I cannot wait, but wait I must, as God still has work for you and me here, as I shall examine in the next chapter.

Eternal Paradox

Into eternity past,
God alone existed;
God the Father,
God the Son, the Word,
And God the Holy Spirit.
There was nothing which existed
Which was not of God.
Nothing, everything
And all things between.

In the beginning,
God, the Word,
Created the heavens and the earth.
There was not anything
Which was created,
Which was not created by God;
All things were created by Him;
Nothing, everything
And all things between.

In the beginning,
The Creation was perfect,
Unspoiled by Sin;
And God said that it was good.
He then created man and woman
And placed them in the garden,
In charge of His Creation.
Nothing, everything
And all things between.

In the midst of the garden,
Stood the tree of knowledge
Of good and evil.
And God commanded,
"Do not eat the fruit thereof
Or you shall surely die."
So they tended the garden;
Nothing, everything
And all things between.

In the garden,
The Serpent came to Eve,
Deceiving her into eating the fruit,
Saying, "You shall be as God
And will never die."
After Eve ate, Adam partook of his own will.
Thus by the first man's sin,
Death fell on everyone and everything
And all things between.

Adam and Eve were
banished by God from the garden.
And the curse of sin fell
On them and all Creation.
But God gave to them
The promise of a Redeemer
Who would vanquish death and the Serpent,
Setting all men free,
No one, everyone,
And everyone between.

In time, God called forth Abraham
From Ur to follow Him.
To honor Abraham's faith,
God established a covenant,
With the promise that
His spiritual descendants
Would outnumber the stars.
No one, everyone
And everyone between.

In God's due time,
He gave His Law to Moses
For the people
To be saved.
But no one could fulfill the Law
God could find not one
Righteous through the Law.
No one and everyone broke the Law
And everyone between.

God also gave
The Promised Land and the Judges,
And the Kings and the Prophets
In order to show the way to Him;
But His people fell deeper
Into disbelief and idolatry,
Further into sin and separation from Him.
No one, everyone
And everyone between.

In the fullness of time,
God at last gave Himself
In the form of His Son, the Word,
The spotless Lamb,
Slain under the Law,
For the sins of the world.
Creator dying for His created,
Dying not for one, but for everyone,
And everyone between.

In the grave He lay
For three days and nights,
Sealed with a stone.
But the Father would not allow
His Holy One to see corruption,
Raising Him to eternal glory,
The first-born of many brethren.
For no one and for everyone
And everyone between.

For as by one man's sin
Death came to all,
By the God-man's death,
Life now comes to all.
For Christ said, "I Am The Way,
The Truth and The Life.
No one comes to the Father
Except by Me."
No one, everyone
And everyone between.

"For I stand at the door
And knock,
And whosoever shall
Invite me in,
With him will I abide forever."
No one, everyone
And everyone between,
Never and for always
And for all time between.

Once more God has entrusted
To man His Creation,
To His Church,
His spotless Bride.
And He has commanded her
To proclaim the Gospel
To every nation, kindred and people.
To no one and to everyone
And to everyone between.

For in God's own time,
Christ, the King, will return
For His Church, His Elect,
More numerous than the stars.
Death, the Curse, the Serpent
Forever vanquished.
Forever, we shall
Live, rule and reign with Him.
Never and for always
And all time between.

During the Age of the Creation
God has wrought His sovereign plan,
To transform created mankind
Into a part of Himself
As the body and Bride of Christ,
His own adopted sons
And joint heirs with Christ.
Forever and for always
And for all time between.

Into eternity future,
God will declare,
"My sovereign will
Is finally complete;
My perfect Creation
Is finally in harmony.
It is well!
Forever and for always
And for all time between."

Mike Carrigan
03-22-2003

Chapter 8

Personal Application

[1] *"The LORD is my shepherd; I shall not want. [2] He maketh me to lie down in green pastures: he leadeth me beside the still waters. [3] He restoreth my soul: he leadeth me in the paths of righteousness for his name's sake. [4] Yea, though I walk through the valley of the shadow of death, I will fear no evil: for thou art with me; thy rod and thy staff they comfort me. [5] Thou preparest a table before me in the presence of mine enemies: thou anointest my head with oil; my cup runneth over. [6] Surely goodness and mercy shall follow me all the days of my life: and I will dwell in the house of the LORD for ever."*

Psalm 23: 1-6

April 3, 2006, dawned as a beautiful, sunny spring morning after a night of severe storms. I said goodbye to my wife and got into my car to drive to work. I pulled out of my driveway and drove less than one mile, when I noticed a fallen cedar tree in a neighbor's yard. Suddenly and without warning, I was jarred by a terrific crash as another car slammed into mine. I was stunned and the world became suddenly surreal. I could feel broken bones and breathlessness and a surge of adrenalin. I was on the razor-thin edge between consciousness and unconsciousness, perhaps between life and death.

I briefly considered the possibility of losing my career and family and recalled the way in which Melynda was killed in a similar accident only a short distance away on the same road. Fear gripped my soul in that awful moment. But I saw in my mind's eye my Lord sitting at the right hand of God interceding for me; and I knew at the same time He was there with me in the car, acting as my Good Shepherd, leading me beside the still waters, setting me in green meadows and bringing me perfect peace as I walked through the valley of the shadow of death. His presence was very real and near. I realized whether I lived or died, that I was in His hand, and nothing else mattered.

I believed then and I believe now that when my time to die does come, I will have that same real peace. In that brief moment, I realized that my relationship with my God was perfect. All of my abilities and talents, my family, my friends, my scientific and intellectual thought and endeavors, my Church, and, yes, even my earthly toils and interpersonal strife and sins were all totally meaningless. I and my life, the good and bad, became nothing in that wonderful moment; and He perfectly became everything. He already was and is; I had just not really known it until then.

I suppose that was the Isaiah moment of my life. Part of me wants to stay in that moment in time, in the temple with God; and in His time, in heaven, that will be the case forever. Just as they were with Isaiah, God and the Holy Spirit and Christ were all with me in that moment, but my experience was of the New Testament vintage; as He was for Isaiah, Christ was the cleansing coals of fire, but for me, Christ was now my Savior and High Priest and Good Shepherd.

And I do want to stay there or go on to heaven, but for now, Romans 12: 1-2 is the guidepost of my life. I have decided that if God was everything for me in that moment, I will strive to leave behind the meaningless things of this world and be transformed by the power of the Holy Spirit to perform God's will and be fruitful in his kingdom.

I will strive to live every day of my life, knowing that He holds them all in His mighty hand, in perfect relationship with my Father and abiding in Christ, so that not one of my precious days will fall as a dead autumn leaf, fruitless, to the cold, hard ground.

God-Given Days

In eternity past,
God already loved me
As he held
The days of my life
In His mighty hand,
Admiring His Creation
As the jeweler
Admires fine pearls.

In my mother's womb,
God knit my bones together,
Stringing the pearls
As the days of my life,
One after the other,
Admiring His Creation
As the potter
Admires his own work.

In my boyhood,
God breathed strength and vigor
Into my soul,
Reeling off the days
As the flutist
Sends notes flying
From his flute,
Weaving them
Into a beautiful melody.

In my youth,
As temptations roared upon me,
God, the Husbandman,
Pruned the shoots of sin
From my life,
Keeping me steadfast and faithful,
And yet humble
In His sight.

In my eagerness,
God also gave me
A life's work
And a young love,
Who was a prophetess
And a teacher unto me.
And He loved and comforted me
When He called her home,
Leading me into new life and hope.

In my loneliness,
He led me beside the still waters
And restored my soul.
In a later day,
He gave me a new love,
A comforter, an encourager,
A companion
In service to Him.

But then!
Another grinding crash!
And shattering glass,
Facing death and life in the balance,
On that day I lived again.
He spared my life, added days.
He was a shield unto me,
The Glory and Lifter of my head.

With this precious gift,
I will serve Him
With a new song
And stronger spirit.
And as He peels away the days
As petals from a rose,
In the center of my heart
He will see Christ.

Mike Carrigan
4-22-06

Chapter 9

God's Blessings

[36] "And one of the Pharisees desired him that he would eat with him. And he went into the Pharisee's house, and sat down to meat. [37] And, behold, a woman in the city, which was a sinner, when she knew that Jesus sat at meat in the Pharisee's house, brought an alabaster box of ointment, [38] And stood at his feet behind him weeping, and began to wash his feet with tears, and did wipe them with the hairs of her head, and kissed his feet, and anointed them with the ointment. [39] Now when the Pharisee which had bidden him saw it, he spake within himself, saying, This man, if he were a prophet, would have known who and what manner of woman this is that toucheth him: for she is a sinner. [40] And Jesus answering said unto him, Simon, I have somewhat to say unto thee. And he saith, Master, say on. [41] There was a certain creditor which had two debtors: the one owed five hundred pence, and the other fifty. [42] And when they had nothing to pay, he frankly forgave them both. Tell me therefore, which of them will love him most? [43] Simon answered and

said, I suppose that he, to whom he forgave most. And he said unto him, Thou hast rightly judged. [44] And he turned to the woman, and said unto Simon, Seest thou this woman? I entered into thine house, thou gavest me no water for my feet: but she hath washed my feet with tears, and wiped them with the hairs of her head. [45] Thou gavest me no kiss: but this woman since the time I came in hath not ceased to kiss my feet. [46] My head with oil thou didst not anoint: but this woman hath anointed my feet with ointment. [47] Wherefore I say unto thee, her sins, which are many, are forgiven; for she loved much: but to whom little is forgiven, the same loveth little. [48] And he said unto her, Thy sins are forgiven."

Luke 7:36-48

God blesses us, His children, in so many wonderful ways, but one of the best is through the gift of family and friends, perhaps most especially through godly spouses. After all the love, sacrifice and growth in a godly marriage are a picture and a foretaste of our relationship with Christ. During the good times we should enrich each other and during the bad times we should assist each other to endure.

Few men have been blessed with two godly wives as have I. They have each blessed me in so many different and varied ways. And even though Melynda and Ruth were sisters, they were given very different personalities by their Father. Melynda, even though obviously human, was really never of this earth; she was born for heaven. She was both ethereal and ephemeral. Her passing from this life, even though heartbreaking for me, was more of a translation than a death. On the other hand Ruth, also a godly woman, is more practical and earthy.

When Melynda and I were married, we were in our early twenties and still maturing as Christians. However, she was ahead of me and taught me so many things about the deeper Christian life including tithing. Melynda loved to give and it was such a blessing for her. I never quite fully understood what so motivated her until one night out of frustration I accused her of giving for the wrong reason: gaining affection which she had not received as a child. (I later asked forgiveness of her and God for this sin.) I learned the deepness and richness of her true motive when she wrote the following note to me based on the story of the grateful woman in Luke:

"Mike, you said I am giving with the wrong purpose: trying to gain affection. This is not so, but please read Luke 7:37-48. **I would deeply express verse 47, 'For she loved much.'** He loved and loves me much. He has forgiven and still forgives much. That is why giving is so important to me. Whatever I give to the Lord is so very little compared to what he first gave to me. But I love much, and giving makes me so happy."

Melynda understood in her heart that giving to God in its purest and deepest and most loving form can never be formula driven or out of a sense of duty but rather only from a cheerful heart filled with love, appreciation and adoration for God and Christ and all that they have done for us first, out of their unmerited love for us.

In her note she also referenced 1 Corinthians, Chapter 9 in which Paul exhorts us to give cheerfully. She understood that God wants to entrust His Kingdom resources to those who will then cheerfully reinvest them in His work thus becoming a veritable fountain of blessing for others.

How many of us understand and practice this kind of motivation for giving today? Certainly Simon the Pharisee did not, and I certainly did not until I saw it modeled and practiced by my wife. I must confess I still do not to the same measure she did. But God so richly blessed me in so many ways by placing Melynda in my life.

Melynda's Song

You came into my life,
One soft summer's day.
Brought there by God,
And in Heaven's sway.

Love was so tender
In the innocence of our youth,
As we shared life together
That's the honest truth.

I was never afraid,
And lived without fear,
Because I lived each day,
Knowing your heart was always near.

Living with you,
I was as happy as a wife could be,
Living and growing,
And just being me.

Over the years,
As you gave me your love;
While content in your care,
I always thanked the Lord above.

Our time together,
Was all too brief.
But my life with you,
Was oh, so sweet!

But as the seasons are carried
On the wings of time,
So must our lives here end
When the clock bell chimes.

God drew my soul to heaven
On the gentle breeze of His voice,
As the leaves of autumn float on the wind
To a place of its choice.

So do not lament for me,
And always remember and never forget;
We shall meet again one day in heaven
Forever together, with our Father and Lord!

Thoughts from 1987
Mike Carrigan

[39] *"He that findeth his life shall lose it: and he that loseth his life for my sake shall find it."*
Matthew 10:39

When Melynda died I was devastated as I noted in the first chapter. But as I stated there, I did believe God had a plan for me and my two young boys. I had a very busy medical practice and faced raising my sons alone. I don't really know if I acted as I often have in a medical crisis, which often demands a resolute and quick action, or out of faith or out of sheer panic and desperation, but I asked Ruth to join me for a period of time to help with the boys.

Only one year before she had completed her BS degree in nursing at the age of 36 and she had been divorced for 10 years. She had steadfastly worked so hard for her degree, and she was working at Vanderbilt Hospital's bone marrow transplant unit. Certainly not out of any sense of secondary gain for herself and not even primarily from a sense of duty, but rather, I believe, from the same deep understanding of giving which had motivated Melynda, Ruth freely decided to give up the life for which she had struggled and to invest it in the lives of her sister's children.

I can't explain it, but as time went on God began to instill in us a sense of deepening respect and admiration and finally love for each other. We were married on June 13, 1988. Ruth has been such a blessing for me over the last 25 years, and I know I have for her also. We have laughed together, we have cried together and we have lived life together. And we have served God together at home and on many foreign medical mission trips. As one of our friends said, "Only God can grow a rose from a rock."

I humbly offer the above examples of how our Father so

mightily loves and blesses us. We should all now use this knowledge as we demonstrate our love for Him in the daily act of cheerfully giving our lives in service for Him in blessing others and in taking the Gospel to the lost. As we have discussed this will facilitate our own sanctification is this life thus preparing us for our eternal relationship with God.

Tribute To Ruth

Your cheeks are like roses,
Your eyes mirrors bright,
Your soul a signet,
Your spirit a light,
Which shines into the cold steel night.

You brighten my day,
You color my way,
You have made my heart soar
Into clouds of joy
From the depths of despair
Because you were there.

Be kind to me and comfort me,
As I will for thee.
This one prayer I pray
That our love will never fade away,
But will last forever and a day!

Mike Carrigan
03-18-1990

Need additional copies?

To order more copies of
God's Purpose in Creation,
contact NewBookPublishing.com

- ❏ Order online at:
  NewBookPublishing.com/Bookstore

- ❏ Call 877-311-5100 or

- ❏ Email Info@NewBookPublishing.com

Reliance Media